My Amazing Body
SENSES

Angela Royston

Raintree
Chicago, Illinois

For more information address the publisher:
Raintree, 100 N. LaSalle, Suite 1200, Chicago IL, 60602

Editorial: Marta Segal Block, Catherine Clarke,
Nick Hunter, Jennifer Mattson
Design: Roslyn Broder, Kim Saar
Illustrations: Will Hobbs
Picture Research: Maria Joannou, Pete Morris
Production: Sal d'Amico, Jonathan Smith
Printed and bound in China by
   South China Printing Company.

08 07 06 05 04
10 9 8 7 6 5 4 3 2 1

Library of Congress Cataloging-in-Publication Data:
Royston, Angela.
  Senses / Angela Royston.
     v. cm. -- (My amazing body)
Includes bibliographical references and index.
Contents: Inside and out -- Why I need my senses --
Seeing -- Blinking
and crying -- Wearing glasses -- Hearing -- Smelling --
Tasting --
Touching -- Feeling heat and cold -- Itching and
aching -- What can go
wrong -- Whole body.
  ISBN 1-4109-0483-0 (lib. bdg.)
  1-4109-0952-2 (paperback)
  1. Senses and sensation--Juvenile literature. [1. Senses
and
sensation.] I. Title. II. Series.
  QP434.R679 2004
  612.8--dc21
                                        2003006728

Acknowledgments
The publishers would like to thank the following for
permission to reproduce photographs:
p. 4 Pete Morris; p. 5 Science Photo Library (Scott
Camazine); p. 6 Alamy Images; p. 7 FLPA (Winfried
Wisniewski); p. 8 Science Photo Library (David Parker);
pp. 10, 20 Science Photo Library (Martin Dohrn); pp. 11,
12, 17, 25 Corbis; p. 13 Getty Images (Digital Vision); p.
14 Photodisc; p. 16 Science Photo Library (Susomo
Nishinaga); p. 18 Science Photo Library (Prof. P. Motta/G.
Franchitto, University "La Sapienza", Rome); p. 19 Gareth
Boden; p. 21 Science Photo Library (Tim Davis); pp. 23,
27 Sally Greenhill; p. 24 FLPA (Silvestris Fotoservice); p.
26 Corbis (Paul A. Souders); p. 28 Bubbles.

Cover image of a brain MRI reproduced with permission
of Science Photo Library/Sovreign. Small image of an eye
reproduced with permission of Science Photo Library and
David Parker.

The publishers would like to thank Carol Ballard for her
assistance in the preparation of this book.

Every effort has been made to contact copyright holders
of any material reproduced in this book. Any omissions
will be rectified in subsequent printings if notice is given
to the publishers.

The paper used to print this book comes from
sustainable resources.

Contents

Any words appearing in bold, **like this,** are explained in the Glossary.

Inside and Out

Seeing, hearing, smelling, tasting, and touching are called your senses. Each sense tells you something about the world around you, and some senses make you aware of things that happen inside your body.

How many senses do you think this girl is using while she eats this orange?

Sense organs

Each sense involves particular parts of the body. For example, you see with your eyes and hear with your ears. Your eyes, ears, nose, mouth, and skin are called **sense organs** and they are on the outside of your body.

The brain is colored yellow in this X ray of a human head. You only see, hear, feel, taste, and smell when your brain receives messages from your sense organs.

Messages to the brain

Each sense organ **reacts** to a certain thing. For example, your eyes react to light. When a sense organ reacts, it sends messages along **nerves** to your brain.

Animal senses

Many animals have sharper senses than people. Many animals can hear sounds that people cannot. Bees can see colors that we cannot.

Why Do I Need My Senses?

Without your senses, you would live in a dark and silent world. You would not be able to feel anything or know when something touched you. You would have no idea where you were or what you needed.

Most important sense

Most people rely on their sense of sight more than any other sense. You use your eyes in almost everything you do—reading, watching television, walking along the street, and even getting dressed.

This girl is using her sense of sight to see her computer, and her sense of touch to work the mouse and hold a book at the same time!

Managing without sight

People who cannot see rely on other senses. **Blind** people use their sense of touch to feel their way. They also listen more carefully to the sounds around them than **sighted** people do.

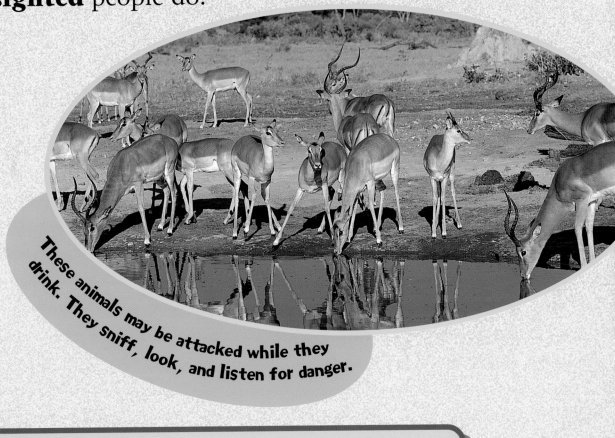

These animals may be attacked while they drink. They sniff, look, and listen for danger.

Extra senses

Animals have the same kind of senses as people, but some animals have an extra sense that helps them to find their way. Some birds fly thousands of miles away when they **migrate,** but they always return to exactly the same place.

Seeing

You see when light enters your eyes. As light bounces off objects, we see their shapes and colors.

How light enters your eyes

In the center of each eye is a round, black hole, called the pupil. Light goes through the pupil into your eye. The colored circle around the pupil is a **muscle** called the iris.

The iris controls how much light can enter your eyes. The front of your eye is protected by a thin, clear covering.

Light enters the eye through the pupil. The iris around the pupil can be brown, blue, gray, or green.

Inside your eye

Behind your pupil is a **lens.** It makes sure that the light forms a clear pattern on your **retina** (back of your eye). Your retina contains **nerve** endings that send messages to your brain. Your brain uses these messages to form an ever-changing picture.

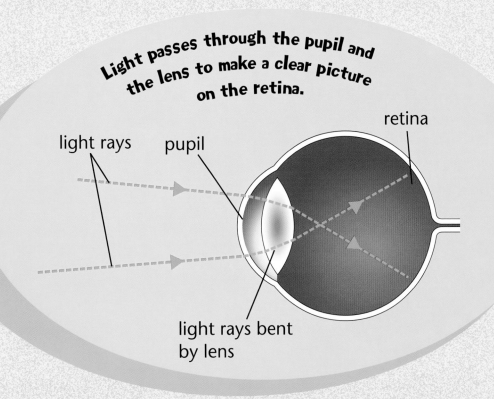

Light passes through the pupil and the lens to make a clear picture on the retina.

light rays

pupil

retina

light rays bent by lens

Eagle-eyed

Birds of **prey,** such as eagles, have extremely good eyesight. An eagle high in the air can spot a tiny beetle moving on the ground way below it.

Blinking and Crying

Your eyes are very **delicate.** Each eye is protected by an eyelid and a layer of salty water that covers the surface.

You close your eyes to shut out light and protect your eyes.

Blinking

You blink every few seconds. Every time you blink, you shut your eyes for an instant. Blinking spreads a fresh film of water across your eyeballs. This keeps them moist and helps to wipe away any dust or **germs** that have gotten into your eyes. You also blink when something touches your eyelashes or comes too close to your eyes.

Tears

If you do get something in your eye, your body makes extra water to wash it out. Normally, the water in your eyes drains into your nose, but this extra water often spills out of your eyes as tears.

Tears flow from our eyes when we are upset or when something irritates the surface of our eyes.

Unblinking stare

Snakes have no eyelids so they cannot blink or close their eyes. Instead, they have a hard see-through cover over their eyes.

Wearing Glasses

Everyone should wear sunglasses to protect their eyes from the harmful rays of bright sunlight. Many people also wear other kinds of glasses to help them see better.

Lenses

Some people do not see clearly because the inside of their eyes do not work as well as they should. Instead of forming a clear picture on the **retina,** some things look blurred. Glasses bend the light to form a clear picture.

Direct sunlight can damage your eyes. Sunglasses protect your eyes, but you should NEVER look directly at the sun, even when you are wearing sunglasses.

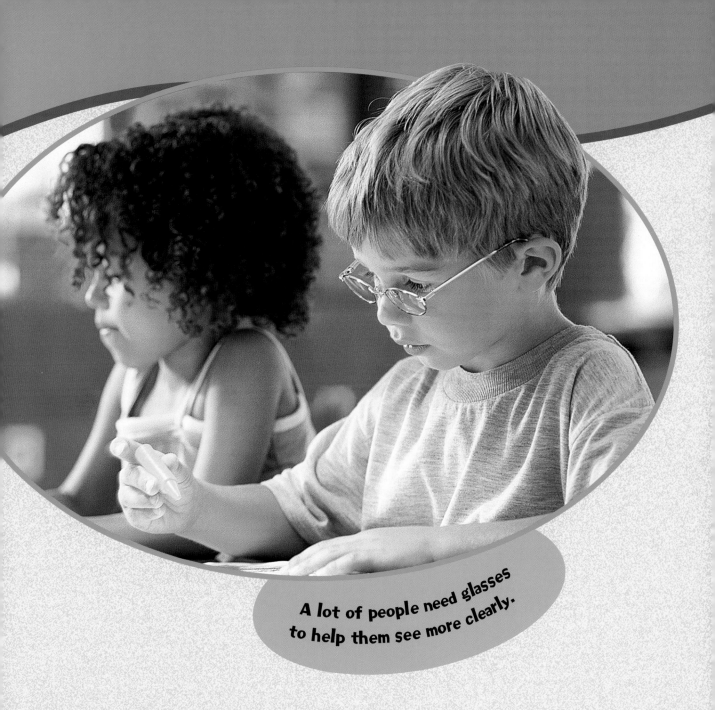

A lot of people need glasses to help them see more clearly.

People who are nearsighted can only see clearly things that are close to them. Their glasses make distant things look clear, too. Some people are farsighted. They can see things that are far away, but not things that are close to them! They have to wear glasses to read or write.

Hearing

When something makes a sound, the air around it ripples with **sound waves.** The waves spread out and may reach your ears. Your ear changes the sound waves into messages that allow you to hear the sound.

Ear flaps

The ears on the side of your head are simply ear flaps. They collect sound and guide it into your ear. Many animals have ear flaps that are much better at collecting sound than ours are. Horses, antelope, and rabbits all have large ear flaps on the tops of their heads. They can also turn their ears to hear even better.

Rabbits and hares use their huge ears to listen out for danger.

Inside an ear

Most of your ear is inside your head. Sounds pass into your ear through your eardrum. They then travel through three small bones and a spiral filled with **liquid** before they reach the **nerves** deep inside your ear.

ear flap

nerve endings

small bones

nerve to brain

eardrum

Your eardrum is made of tight skin. Sounds pass through it into your ear. The nerves that react to sounds are deep inside your ears.

Bats

Some bats use their ears like radar to find their way in the dark. They make high-pitched squeaks that echo, or bounce back, off objects. Hearing the echo tells the bats where things are.

Smelling

You can smell some things even though they are far away from you. This is because tiny **particles**, which are too small to see, float into the air and reach your nose. **Nerve** endings in your nose **react** to the particles and send messages to your brain about the smell.

Inside your nose

The nerve endings that react to smells are right at the top of the inside of your nose. The more particles that reach your nose, the stronger the smell.

Tiny hairs in your nose trap dirt and dust from the air you breathe in. In this picture some of the hairs have been magnified many times and colored yellow and orange.

To smell something better, you sniff. Sniffing draws in more air and pulls it higher up your nose to the nerve endings.

Telling smells apart

Some smells are pleasant and some are disgusting. No one knows how the nerve endings in your nose tell one smell from another, but your brain decides which smells you like and dislike.

Animal noses

Some dogs can smell so well they can track a person from the smell of their footprints. Dogs can smell much better than humans can because their whole nose is lined with nerve endings. Police train dogs to sniff out illegal **drugs.**

Tasting

To taste something, you lick it or swirl it around your mouth. If food tastes bad or rotten, you spit it out and don't swallow it. When food tastes good, though, you want to eat more of it.

Taste buds

You can taste because your tongue and mouth have taste buds containing **nerve** endings. When **particles** of food or **liquid** reach these nerve endings, they send messages to your brain about the taste.

This is what the surface of your tongue looks like, magnified by almost 200 times its real size! The yellow-orange area in the middle shows some taste buds.

Kinds of taste

Although you taste many different flavors, your taste buds sense only four main tastes— sweet, salty, sour, and bitter. Every flavor is made up of a mixture of these main tastes. The tastes most people like best are salty and sweet. Lemons taste sour while pure chocolate tastes bitter. Chocolate is mixed with sugar to make it taste sweeter.

When you eat food like this Chinese meal, you can taste a lot of different flavors.

Smell and taste

Your sense of taste relies on your sense of smell. When you have a cold and your nose is blocked, you cannot smell. Food becomes less tasty, too.

Touching

You rely mainly on your skin to give you a sense of touch. **Nerve** endings in your skin send messages to your brain. Some nerve endings tell you what things feel like. Others tell you whether something is hot or cold, and others make you feel pain.

Sensitivity

Some parts of your skin are more **sensitive** than other parts. Your fingertips, the tip of your tongue, your lips, and the soles of your feet are particularly sensitive to touch. This is because they contain more nerve endings than other parts of your body.

Your fingertips are sensitive to touch. The skin has ridges and contains many nerve endings that react to touch.

Using touch

You usually use your fingertips to tell you how something feels. It may feel rough or smooth, hard or soft. Your fingertips are so sensitive they can feel even tiny bumps.

A cat's fur feels soft and smooth and is nice to touch and pet.

Cat's whiskers

A cat's whiskers are sensitive to touch. The cat uses them to feel its way in the dark. The whiskers are attached to nerves in the skin.

Feeling Heat and Cold

Different **nerves** in your skin **react** to heat and to cold. These nerves only react when something hot or cold touches your skin. You can feel the heat of a candle flame without touching it, because the flame heats the air around it, which touches your skin. Some parts of your body are more **sensitive** to heat and cold than other parts.

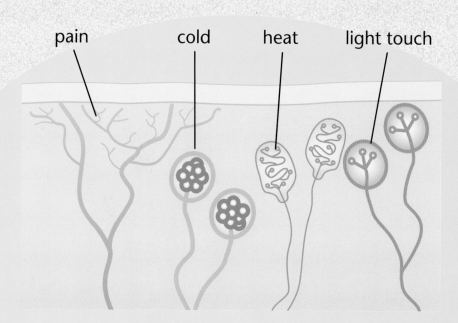

pain   cold   heat   light touch

This diagram shows some of the different nerves in your skin that sense things like heat, cold, and pain.

Lips and tongue

Your tongue and the inside of your mouth are easily burned by hot food or drinks. Because your lips are particularly sensitive to heat and cold, they check how hot something is before you put it in your mouth.

Testing bath water

Your feet are more sensitive to hot and cold than your hands are. Water may feel warm to your hand but too hot for your feet. Use your elbow, which is also sensitive to heat, to test how hot your bath water is.

This mother uses her elbow to test how hot her baby's bath water is.

Snakes

Some snakes use heat to find mice or other **prey** in the dark. Special nerve endings on the snake's head sense the heat from other animals' bodies.

Itching and Aching

Different **nerves** in your skin **react** to different kinds of touch. Some nerves react to itching. Other nerves react to pain.

Itching

The surface of your skin is so **sensitive** you can feel even a light touch. When your skin itches, you usually scratch it until it stops itching. You should not scratch insect bites, rashes, or chicken pox spots, however, because scratching them can damage the skin and they may become **infected.**

This dog is scratching an itch behind his ear. Animals feel itches and pain, just like humans do.

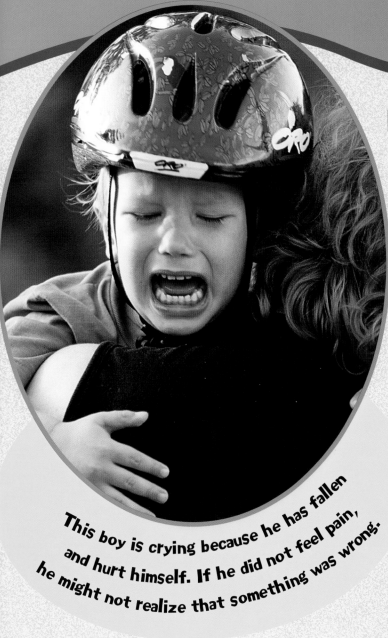

This boy is crying because he has fallen and hurt himself. If he did not feel pain, he might not realize that something was wrong.

Pain

You feel pain when your skin is damaged, perhaps by heat or by being hit. Pain is important because it tells you that something is wrong. You also have nerves in other parts of your body to tell you about pain. You may sometimes get a stomachache, for example, or a headache.

Stopping pain

Some **drugs,** such as aspirin, help to lessen the feeling of pain. An anesthetic is a drug that takes away your whole sense of touch, not just of pain.

What Can Go Wrong?

Things can sometimes go wrong with the **nerves** and the **sense organs.** If your senses don't fully work, it affects your entire life.

Losing your sense of touch

When you have been kneeling for a long time, your legs may go numb. This is because you have squashed the nerves in the skin. The nerves quickly recover, but tingle uncomfortably as they do so. If you have an accident that damages the nerves in your spine, they may not recover. This means you would be unable to feel anything in part of your body.

This man cannot feel anything in his legs and feet because the nerves have been badly damaged, but it doesn't stop him from playing tennis.

Blindness and deafness

Most **blind** people can see some light and dark, but not enough to tell what things are.

People are deaf when their ears do not work properly. Some deaf people are able to understand what people are saying by watching the shapes their lips make as they speak.

This blind woman is using a stick to feel the ground in front of her.

Color blind

People are color-blind when they cannot tell all the different colors apart. Many animals, including cats, are color-blind. They see most colors as shades of gray.

The Whole Body

You could do almost nothing without your senses. You could perhaps lie still and breathe, but eating would be difficult if you could not feel the food in your mouth.

Moving around

You use your **muscles** and bones to move your body, but you would not know where to move without your senses. You have to be able to feel something to pick it up—and you need your sense of touch to know when it is in your hand.

These children are bouncing and having fun. They are using their eyes and ears, as well as their muscles and brains.

Using your brain

All the information collected by your senses is sent to your brain. Your brain uses it to decide what to do.

When someone throws you a ball, for example, you use your eyes to track its path and guide your hands into the right position to catch it. It would be very difficult for people and animals to survive without their senses.

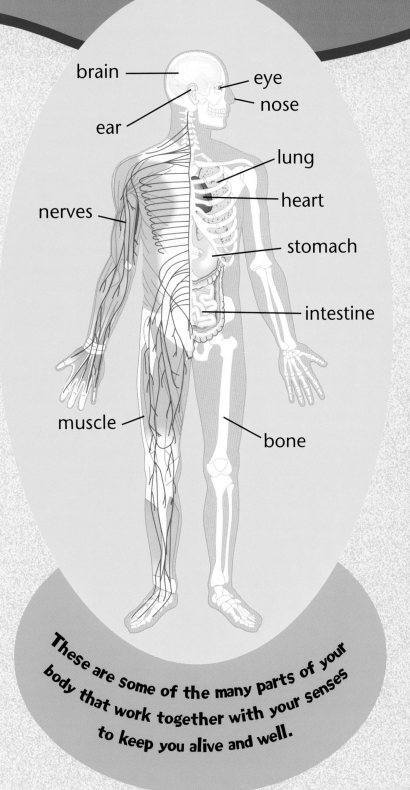

brain

eye

nose

ear

lung

heart

nerves

stomach

intestine

muscle

bone

These are some of the many parts of your body that work together with your senses to keep you alive and well.

Find Out for Yourself

Everybody's body is slightly different but they all work in the same way. Find out more about how your own amazing body works by noticing what happens to it. When you are blindfolded, can you tell what different tastes are? How well can you see in the dark? Does water feel hotter to your feet or to your hand? You will find the answers to many of your questions in this book, but you can also use other books and the Internet.

Books to read

Royston, Angela. *Why Do I Get a Toothache? And Other Questions About Nerves*. Chicago: Heinemann Library, 2002.

Hartley, Karen. *The Sixth Sense and Other Special Senses*. Chicago: Heinemann, 2000.

Hartley, Karen. *Senses*. Chicago: Heinemann, 2001.

Using the Internet

Explore the Internet to find out more about your senses. Websites can change, so if some of the links below no longer work, don't worry. Use a search engine, such as www.yahooligans.com or www.internet4kids.com and type in keywords such as "senses," "seeing," and "hearing."

Websites

www.kidshealth.org contains lots of information about how your body works and how to stay healthy.

www.brainpop.com click on "health" for quizzes and films about different parts of the body, including your senses.

Disclaimer

All the Internet addresses (URLs) given in this book were valid at the time of going to press. However, due to the dynamic nature of the Internet, some addresses may have changed, or sites may have ceased to exist since publication. While the author and publishers regret any inconvenience this may cause readers, no responsibility for any such changes can be accepted by either the author or the publishers.

Glossary

blind unable to see

delicate easily damaged

drug chemical that affects the body or brain. Medical drugs are used to treat illnesses. Harmful drugs that can damage the body are illegal.

germ tiny form of life that can make you ill. Germs are so small that you need a microscope to see them.

infect bring in germs

lens curved piece of glass or other see-through material that changes the direction of rays of light

liquid flowing substance that is not a gas or a solid. Water is a liquid.

microscope instrument that makes very tiny things look large enough to see

migrate move to a warmer place for part of the year

muscle part of the body that you use to move your bones

nerve fiber that carries messages from the sense organs to the brain. Another kind of nerve carries messages from the brain to the muscles.

particle very tiny piece of something

prey animal that is caught and eaten by another animal

react to respond to

retina back of the eye

sense organ part of the body that reacts to either light, sound, chemicals, or touch to produce one of the senses

sensitive easily affected

sighted able to see

sound wave movements in the air that your ears respond to when you hear sounds

X ray kind of photograph that shows parts of the inside of your body, such as your bones or brain

Index